Tattoos and Indigenous Peoples

Judith Levin

ROSEN
PUBLISHING®

New York

For Ryan Flanagan (and his tattoos)

Published in 2009 by The Rosen Publishing Group, Inc.
29 East 21st Street, New York, NY 10010

Library of Congress Cataloging-in-Publication Data

Levin, Judith (Judith N.), 1956–
Tattoos and indigenous peoples / Judith Levin. — 1st ed.
    p. cm.—(Tattooing)
Includes bibliographical references and index.
ISBN-13: 978-1-4042-1828-4 (library binding)
1. Tattooing—History—Juvenile literature. 2. Indigenous peoples—Juvenile literature. I. Title.
GN419.3.L48 2009
391.6'5—dc22

                                          2007050753

Manufactured in Malaysia
On the cover: Top: This Maori chief from New Zealand is wearing traditional tattoos. Bottom: In 2003, a woman from Samoa gets a traditional tattoo in New Zealand.

Contents

INTRODUCTION

When "tribal" tattoos began to be fashionable in the 1980s, people admired them for their bold black patterns. They look different from the older American heart and anchor tattoos or the realistic, colorful images that are also popular.

Many tribal tattoos are based on designs from islands in the Pacific Ocean, including Samoa, New Zealand, Hawaii, and Borneo. But if you could go back in time, you would find many more styles of tribal tattoos. In the late 1800s, the English naturalist Charles Darwin wrote in his book *The Descent of Man*, "Not one great country can be named, from the polar regions in the north to New Zealand in the south, in which the aborigines do not tattoo themselves."

Indigenous Peoples

Darwin used the word "aborigines." These are the "indigenous" peoples of the title of this book. They are also called Native Peoples, American Indians or Native Americans (in the United States), and First Nations (in Canada). Indigenous peoples are the cultural groups and their descendants who lived in a region before it was discovered and taken over by another people.

Tribal-style tattoos are admired for their bold patterns and, for some people, are seen as a way to connect to an older, simpler way of life.

Many of these indigenous peoples were tribal. They lived in extended family groups, not modern nations.

"Indigenous" means "having originated in a place." If you want a garden that's easy to take care of, you plant flowers and trees that are indigenous, or native, to the climate of your backyard. But people, and human cultures, are more complicated than plants. People can adapt. If you're cold, you put on clothes. If you've got pale skin, you use sunscreen. Unlike plants, the adaptations of indigenous peoples to their native land are not usually biological. Instead they are cultural: indigenous peoples have traditional ways of life that were developed over long periods of time. They understand and make good use of the resources offered by their native land.

Bloodthirsty Savages and the Noble Savages

In the past, indigenous peoples have been called "savages," "barbarians," and "heathens." Those old names show that these people were considered less civilized, and even less human, than those of the nations that "discovered" and conquered them.

Other philosophers, writers, and artists have spoken of the "noble savage" instead of the "bloodthirsty savage," believing that indigenous peoples live simpler, better, more natural lives than modern people do. But to see indigenous peoples as all bad, all good, or even all alike is to ignore how different these people are from one another.

This habit of lumping indigenous peoples together is an old one. Early anthropologists called them "primitive." They believed that by studying these peoples, they could understand what "early man"—Stone Age people—were like. They believed that there is a natural growth in cultures. Just as a child becomes an adult, a primitive culture is one that hasn't grown up yet.

In the late 1800s and early 1900s, the American anthropologist Franz Boas and his students Margaret Mead and Ruth Benedict said that if people believe that all cultures are going to grow up to be like theirs, then they are saying that the "civilized" people are the best, the most advanced, and the most valuable. (Eastern cultures such as those of Japan and China have each made the same claim for themselves. It isn't just Europeans and Americans.) Also, Boas said, there is no proof that one kind of culture "grows" into another—or that it wants to.

What people had been doing, said Boas, was linking "civilization" with technology. Some indigenous peoples had more advanced technology and science than outsiders realized. The Polynesians traveled thousands of miles across the Pacific Ocean, long before Europeans could do it. But most indigenous cultures do not build great monuments or factories. Instead, they develop in other ways. Anthropologists have discovered that these cultures have spent a long time—sometimes thousands of years—creating stories and rituals and arts. In many places, these arts included tattooing—not just the designs but also the rituals surrounding the giving of a tattoo.

What Indigenous Tattoos Mean

Much of what anthropologists might once have been able to find out about tattoo traditions has been lost. Conquerors, mission-aries, and colonial governments destroyed the traditions of the people whose land they took. Native peoples died defending their land and from diseases brought by the Europeans.

Still, as you look at the tattoo traditions of indigenous peoples, you can think about those who created them. Instead

The Head of a Chief of New Zealand, the face curiously tataow'd, or mark'd, according to their Manner.

When Captain James Cook sailed to the Pacific Islands in the late 1700s, his ship's artist, Sydney Parkinson, drew this portrait of a native chief in New Zealand.

of just looking for designs you like, you can ask what these tattoos meant to the people who first wore them. These tattoos were a way of communicating. They said to other people in the same group, "I am old enough to get married" or "I am brave enough to be a hunter." They said to others in the region, "Hands off! This person belongs to us." They said to gods or helpful spirits, "I ask for your help and your protection" or "This tattoo marks the part of my body that hurts. Could you make it stop hurting?" They said, "By getting this tattoo, I show that I am one of Us"—part of a particular family or tribe, part of the group of people who fished or who could kill large animals. Often, they said, "This is what we think beauty is. We make ourselves fully human by decorating ourselves like this."

When people decorate their bodies today with clothes, hairstyles, jewelry, or body art such as makeup, piercings, or tattoos, they are communicating. People show who they are. They also show who they *don't* want to be—their parents, maybe, or like other kids at school. They follow social rules that they might not even know are there. There is only a short list of occasions to which a boy wears a dress. You can't go to your brother's wedding dressed only in your underwear. But you can play with what your clothes and body art say. You can wear designer knock-offs and pretend to have more money than you really have. You can mix up tattoos from different cultures.

The way people today communicate with body decorations and the way traditional cultures communicate with tattoos are the same in some ways and different in others. The tattoo is permanent—really permanent in a world without surgeons—and there is very little that people can pretend. In most indigenous cultures, other people pretty much know who your parents are and who you are. You express your individuality. In a traditional culture, people reveal their place in their community. In some places, that information is inscribed on their bodies. The tattoos break open their skin, which is the boundary between themselves and the world. They shed blood, which is a symbol of life and death. Who they are is written upon them for the rest of their lives.

CHAPTER 1

Prehistoric Tattoos

Tattooing is an ancient art. It is so old that the earliest tattoos archaeologists know about are older than the invention of writing (around 3500 BCE) or even farming (10,000 BCE). They are prehistoric, from before history could be recorded.

The Oldest Tattoos

Archaeologists have discovered tools in France, Portugal, and Scandinavia that were probably used for tattooing. These are at least 12,000 years old, from the time of the last Ice Age. They found clay dishes and red ochre (a natural red or yellow pigment) and sharp bone tools shaped like big needles without the eye. In the same places, archaeologists discovered small statues in the shape of the human figure that are engraved with abstract geometric designs.

Ötzi the Iceman

In 1991, hikers discovered the frozen body of a man in the mountains near the border of Italy

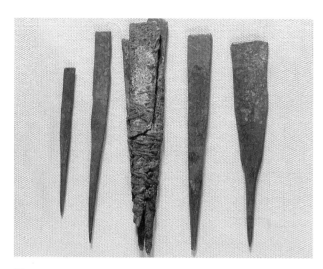

These small bronze tattooing tools from about 1450 BCE were excavated in Egypt.

and Austria. "Ötzi," as scientists named him, turned out to be more than five thousand years old. His body had been preserved in a glacier soon after his death, so his skin, bones, internal organs, clothing, and tools were all literally frozen in time. On his skin are the oldest tattoos that have been preserved. Ötzi has a black cross tattooed on the inside of his left knee, six straight lines on his lower back, and many parallel lines on his ankles, legs, and wrist. His tattoos were not for decoration. His clothing would have hidden them, and they do not make a pattern. When scientists X-rayed his body, they discovered evidence of joint disease under each tattoo. This revelation suggests that the tattoos were meant to relieve pain.

Ancient Egyptian Tattoos

Before the discovery of Ötzi, the oldest known tattooed mummies were Egyptian ones from around 2000 BCE. The mummified body of the priestess Amunet is tattooed with parallel lines on her arms and thighs and a pattern of curved parallel lines below her belly button. Even older statues show female figures with marks—believed to be tattoos—on their thighs.

The oldest tattoo that shows a picture rather than a geometric design is also Egyptian. The god Bes, who took the form of a dwarf and whose face looked like a mask, was linked to women and children, and was found tattooed on some female mummies. Bes was the god of women in labor and would protect them during this time of danger. The archaeologists who discovered the mummies believed that Bes was meant to frighten evil spirits away and would thus drive away pain and

A young Egyptian woman plays a lute on this pottery bowl from about 1400–1300 BCE. On her right thigh is a tattoo of the dwarf god Bes.

misfortune. Some of the mummies have the tattoo of Bes and also a tattooed pattern of dots across the abdomen, like a net. As the woman's abdomen grew bigger during pregnancy, the "net" would expand and protect her.

Pazyryk Mummies

The Pazyryks were tribal nomads and warriors who lived in the steppes of eastern Europe and western Asia from the sixth through the second centuries BCE. They dominated the region because they rode horses, and most peoples at that time did not have them.

In 1948, a Russian anthropologist named Sergei Ivanovich Rudenko excavated tombs about 120 miles (193 kilometers) north of the modern border between Russia and China. In the tomb, he found jewelry, musical instruments, pipes, fabrics from Persia and China, many pieces of riding gear, and the heavily tattooed body of a man. In 1993, the body of a tattooed Pazyryk woman was found in Siberia. Theirs are among the most detailed and beautiful tattoos found from this early period. The man has a pattern of intertwined animals tattooed on his legs, arms, and shoulders. These include fish, deer, rams, and what look like imaginary beasts. The woman's tattoos are similar and include a tattooed "bracelet" of antlers on her wrist.

Only two of the Pazyryk bodies that were found had these tattoos, and both were buried with beautiful and expensive objects. This discovery shows that tattoos were worn by

This Pazyryk woman's mummified body, which is about 2,400 years old, preserved her elaborate clothing and her beautiful tattoos as well.

people of high status. Archaeologists cannot know for certain what these tattoos meant. In parts of Asia, tattoos of animals were used to protect the wearer during battles and activities such as hunting and fishing. Certainly, the tattoos were meant to be beautiful. In addition, the man also has a row of tiny circles tattooed down his spine. These do not look like decorations but were probably meant to cure back pain.

CHAPTER 2

Marks of Pride, Marks of Shame

Prehistoric tattoos were meant to help or honor the people who wore them. Greek and Roman historians had a different understanding of what tattoos meant. When Herodotus (fifth century BCE) described the Scythians, a tribe that lived at the same time of the Pazyryks, he said they were bloodthirsty savages who scalped their enemies. In the third century CE, a Roman historian, Herod of Antioch, wrote, "The Britons incise on their bodies colored pictures of animals, of which they are very proud." In the seventh century, the Picts were tattooed with blue designs made from a plant called woad.

The Ancient Greeks and Romans

For the ancient Greeks and Romans, tattoos showed that tribal peoples were barbarians. They believed that it was savage and uncivilized to mark the human body. Yet, the Greeks learned to tattoo slaves and criminals. The Romans tattooed the foreheads of slaves who

Painting in the sixteenth century, John White was more than one thousand years too late to know what the ancient Picts of Great Britain really looked like. In White's perception of the ancient Picts, he shows a warrior who has blue tattoos of birds, animals, and serpents.

tried to escape with the letters *fug,* short for the Latin word for "fugitive." The ninth century CE Greek emperor Theophilus punished two monks by having obscene poetry tattooed on their foreheads.

For the Greeks and Romans, tattoos were marks of shame, not honor. Their word for tattoo—*stigmates*—gives us the English word "stigma": something that sets someone apart and shows that he or she has been disgraced. The power to tattoo someone against his or her will is the power to violate that person.

China and Japan

In 200 BCE, the Yue people of China wore tattoos of mythical beasts to protect themselves while fishing. In the 1600s, indigenous women of Hainan Island, southeast of China, wore tattooed flowers and butterflies on their faces. Their tradition said that a young woman had her hand tattooed when she got engaged. On the evening before the wedding, the man she would marry tattooed the signs of his family on her face.

Among the Ainu people, an indigenous people living on the northern Japanese islands, women wore tattoos around their mouths, arms, and hands. Such tattoos, which covered the area around their mouths and turned up at the edges, showed that they were married.

Other tattoo traditions also existed among the Japanese and Chinese, but by 500 BCE, many of the Chinese had begun to follow the teachings of the philosopher Confucius. He taught

A small stone sculpture from the third century BCE depicts a Chinese man *(right)* wearing tattoos on his face. A few hundred years later, the philosopher Confucious discouraged tattooing.

that the human body was a gift from one's parents and ancestors. He believed, as the Greeks and Romans did, that the human body must not be maimed or marked. Like the Greeks and Romans, educated Chinese said that tattooing was "barbaric." But they, too, began to use tattoos to mark slaves and criminals. When they forced farmers to join the army, they tattooed them so that they could not run back to their villages.

From Shame to Pride

Because tattoos were used so widely as punishment, they began to take on a new meaning. Soldiers and people who

An Early Recipe for Removing Tattoos

The ancient Greeks and Romans wrote down recipes for the tattoo ink they used. They also created the first method of removing (or at least blurring) a tattoo that archaeologists know about. The recipe called for applying mixtures of such substances as "the scum on the bottom of the chamber pot" and strong vinegar or pigeon poop mixed with vinegar. Bound to the skin for a long time, these ingredients would have caused enough irritation to make sure that many layers of skin became infected and fell off.

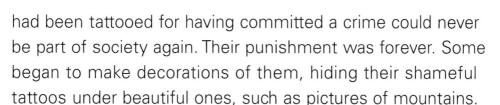

had been tattooed for having committed a crime could never be part of society again. Their punishment was forever. Some began to make decorations of them, hiding their shameful tattoos under beautiful ones, such as pictures of mountains.

In Japan, tattoos were also used as punishment. A lower-class criminal had the Japanese word meaning "bad" or "evil" tattooed on his forehead. Some Japanese also hid their mark of shame with a mark of beauty, such as a flower.

Other Chinese and Japanese people who had been tattooed formed gangs. A novel called *Shuihu (Outlaws of the Marsh)* told the story of 108 outlaws who defy a cruel government and help ordinary people. It was published in the 1500s in China and

This Japanese woodblock print from 1811 CE by artist Hokusai shows a famous warrior, Tametomo, defeating two enemies who, even together, cannot pull the string of his giant bow.

was later translated into Japanese. The tattoos of some bandits gave them special powers, like great skill in fighting.

Tattoos were never socially acceptable, but they did become popular. Between 1603 and 1868, Japan was closed to outsiders. During this time, the art of making pictures from woodblock prints was perfected. Inexpensive but beautiful pictures of cities, land-scapes, warriors, and women became available. The style of these prints, and the technique of printing one color at a time from wooden blocks, led to the Japanese style of tattoo. These tattoos are complex, realistic, and colorful and make a single picture—for instance dragons, warriors, or cherry blossoms—over much of a person's body. Firefighters, fishermen, and other people with dangerous jobs had guardian tattoos to protect them.

Yet, tattooing was still more or less discouraged in Japan, even after Westerners began to travel there in the late 1900s to be tattooed by Japan's great artists. The full-body tattoo became the mark of the *yakuza*, Japanese organized crime.

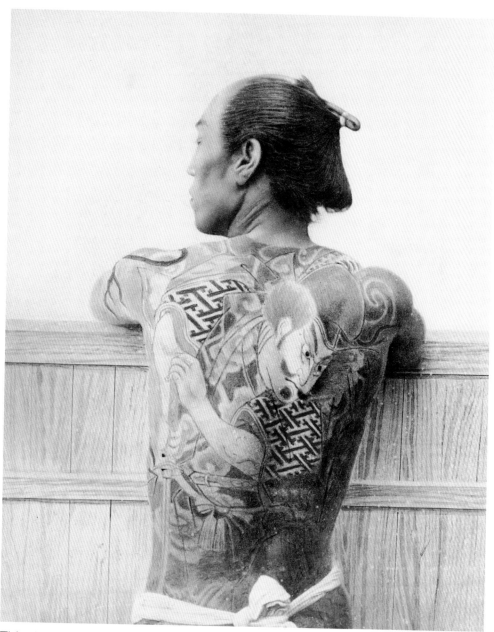

This Japanese man was photographed in the 1880s displaying his elaborate, multicolored (and illegal) tattoo. Its subject and style are clearly influenced by the woodblock prints of the same period.

Jews and Christians

In 1930, the English archaeologist Leonard Woolley excavated small painted statues in the area between the Tigris and Euphrates rivers, in what is now Iraq. This region, which the Greeks called Mesopotamia, contained the ancient civilization that developed the first writing in the world and the first cities. On these figurines, Woolley found designs that he believed showed body painting and tattooing and/or the decorative designs of scars called cicatrices. An indigenous culture of tattoos existed in Iraq until the twentieth century.

Many people have been told that the Hebrew Bible says that people shouldn't get tattoos or make ritual scars. "You shall not make any cuttings in your flesh for the dead, or print any marks upon yourself" (Leviticus 19:28). The biblical Jews shared a cultural background with the Arabs of the region. They are all Semitic peoples, sharing a common cultural background and related languages. The laws about tattooing in the Bible have been interpreted in different ways. They may tell us that the Jews of that period tattooed themselves and made cuts in their flesh to mourn the dead and were being told to stop. Or, they were being told to make new, different marks instead. In the religious ceremony of circumcision, a ritual cutting is performed—a kind of ritual cutting that, like tattoos, identifies the people of one group.

The early Christians also made laws about tattoos. In the fourth century, Saint Basil the Great wrote that Christians must not grow their hair long or tattoo themselves like "the heathen."

According to *Tattoo History: A Source Book*, edited by Steve Gilbert, a later ruling from a council of bishops in England in 787 said that Christians were "to be greatly praised" for getting tattoos "for the sake of God" but must not "be tattooed for superstitious reasons in the manner of the heathen," like the native peoples of England. Tattoos were still being used to identify which group of people someone belonged to.

Over time, the practice of tattooing among Christians and in Europe largely died out. Still, some people had them. King Harold II of England died in the Battle of Hastings in 1066. After that battle, the English-speaking Saxons of Briton lost control of the country to William the Conqueror and the Normans (French). King Harold's body was unrecognizable, except that on his chest was tattooed the name of his wife and the name of his country. In the eleventh through thirteenth centuries, Crusaders and pilgrims to Jerusalem and the Holy Land got tattoos there as souvenirs of their journeys. These often included crosses or other Christian symbols, their initials, and the date. When later Europeans saw tattoos in other parts of the world, they recognized them because they had seen the tattoos of Christian pilgrims.

CHAPTER 3

Tattoo Traditions and the European Age of Exploration

The words and images Europeans inked into their skin were not called tattoos. They were called "pricked drawings." The word "tattoo" came into the English language from the Tahitian people after the English explorer Captain James Cook encountered them in 1768 during his travels in the Pacific Ocean. The Tahitian word was *tatau*.

Cook's voyages in the late 1700s were just part of the vast exploration and conquest of other continents by Europeans after Christopher Columbus (1451–1506). The ability to cross oceans brought Europeans in contact with new peoples. These included the peoples of North, South, and Central America; the many islands in the Pacific Ocean, including New Zealand and Australia; and Africa. Travel across the Atlantic brought Europeans into contact with many indigenous cultures—and their tattoos.

The Europeans Encounter Tattoos

The Europeans were not looking for cultures to explore or for tattoos. They wanted faster trade routes to India and the Far East. They were looking for El Dorado, the mythical land of gold. Some were also interested in science and in "curiosities." Naturalists collected new plants and animals (for example, corn, tomatoes, giraffes, and turkeys). Sometimes, they "collected" people and brought them back, too. In 1566, a Dutch ship captain captured an Inuit woman and her child and exhibited her, advertising that she had permanent blue pictures on her face. Also in the 1500s, the Spanish conquistadors who invaded South and Central America were amazed by the tattoos on the indigenous peoples they saw there.

Unlike many captains of the eighteenth century, James Cook was an explorer. He and his crew members were interested in unknown plants and animals, unusual rock formations, and the many indigenous peoples they encountered, especially those who were "tatowed."

Polynesian Tattoo Traditions

For most indigenous cultures, the coming of Westerners ended traditional tattooing. In some of the Polynesian islands, tattooing survived.

Polynesia is a group of islands that form a huge triangle in the Pacific Ocean. Each side of the triangle is 4,000 miles (6,437 km) long. The northern point of the triangle is Hawaii, the eastern point is Easter Island, and the southern point is New Zealand. In modern times, these islands belong to different countries, but the indigenous peoples of Polynesia speak languages that are related to one another. The word for tattooist is *tufuga* in Samoan, *tohunga* in New Zealand, and *kahuna* in Hawaii.

Between about 3000 and 1000 BCE, people set out in boats from what is now Taiwan. They settled on islands in the Pacific—Micronesia and Melanesia, which had their own populations. Between 1300 and 900 BCE, they traveled farther, settling on the islands now known as Fiji, Samoa, and Tonga. Between 200 and 600 CE, they settled Tahiti, the Marquesas, Easter Island, and the islands of Hawaii. Some time around 1000 CE, they populated New Zealand. As these people migrated, they brought with them their language, style of decorating pottery, and tradition of making tattoos.

Samoa Saves Its Traditions

The United States, Great Britain, and Germany eventually claimed the islands of Polynesia. When these governments reached an agreement about who controlled what, western Samoa belonged to Germany. The Germans were more interested in traditional customs than some other nations.

Members of the German government on Samoa had themselves tattooed by native artists.

In addition, the Samoans had resisted the missionaries. The Samoans believed they could add the beliefs of Catholicism to their own traditional beliefs but also keep their old gods and traditions. Although the missionaries said that tattooing was the work of the devil, tattooing was too important to their culture for them to abandon it.

In Samoa, tattooing was a rite of passage, which is a ritual that marks the change from one social status to another. In Samoa, a boy who did not get tattooed at puberty could not become a man. He would be a man biologically, in his body, but he would not be a man *culturally*. No matter how big and strong he was, he could not marry and had to remain silent when the men were speaking, like a boy. A man could not become a chief without a tattoo. Samoan young men with tattoos refused to go to the missionaries' schools with "cowardly" untattooed boys.

The Ritual of Tattooing

At puberty, a boy would be tattooed by a *tufuga*. The tufuga learned his craft over many years, usually from his father. For practice, he would make tattoo patterns in sand or on cloth. His tools were made of sharpened bones or boar's teeth held together with a piece of turtle's shell and attached to a wood or bone handle, and a mallet.

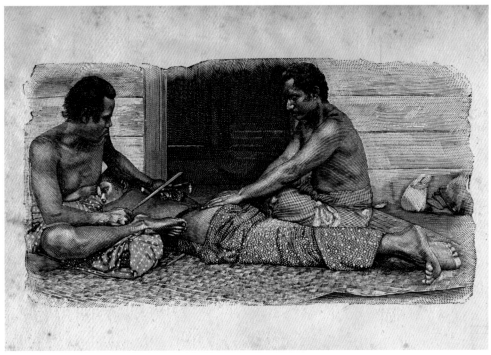

In the 1870s, young men on Samoa were still tattooed in the traditional way. Receiving the *pe'a*, or pattern of the tattoo, could take many months and was very painful.

Boys being tattooed were not supposed to show that they were in pain. It was a time to show fortitude. But they did not have to suffer alone. Sometimes, two boys would agree to be tattooed together. When it was time for a chief's son to be tattooed, the chief would invite the village boys of the right age to be tattooed at the same time. He would pay for the work of the tufugas, which was expensive, and for the other parts of the ceremony. He gave the young men gifts to thank them for sharing his son's pain.

To help the boys, friends and relatives would sing to them. The tufuga himself would sing for a chief's son. Carl Marquardt, writing a book about tattooing in Samoa in 1899, said the tunes of the songs were monotonous, which would make them soothing. The songs had many verses. Listening to the words and being lulled by the monotonous tunes would help take the boys' mind off their pain. The singing also reminded them that they were not alone. Their people were there to keep them company and to see if they were brave.

The patterns of the tattoos given to Samoan boys were complex and detailed. The pattern is called the *pe'a*. That is the word for a kind of local animal, sometimes described as a bat, sometimes as a flying fox. In Samoan myths, the pe'a is a guardian. For the tattoo, the animal's "wings" are wrapped around the man's legs. It looks like the man is wearing pants to his knees. On Tonga, islanders told sailors from Captain Cook's ship that the pe'a would protect warriors during battle.

The tufuga would stop working at dusk or when the young men could no longer bear the pain. Only an area about the size of a man's hand could be tattooed in one day. At the end of each day, the people who had watched danced, wrestled, and boxed. They staged sham fights. The tattoo process might continue for months because the tufuga could not work every day. He gave the boys time to recover.

The zigzagging stripes that went from the area around the pelvis and around the legs may be an image of a millipede, an animal that appears in Samoan myths. It is associated with death or with surviving an illness. On the abdomen may be the

Samoan tattoo artists still prefer their traditional hand tools to modern machines. This close-up view shows a tattooist applying part of a traditional full-body tattoo to another Samoan.

image of a boat, in memory of the long voyage taken by the Samoan's ancestors. The last part "locked" the design at the belly button. As a baby's birth ends with the cutting of the umbilical cord that binds it to its mother, the end of the child's life as a boy ends with the tattooing of the navel.

When the tattoo was finished, the family threw a party. The tufuga smashed a water vessel at the feet of the young man who had just been tattooed—a symbol of cleansing or of birth. During the long healing process, the young man had trouble even sitting down. His family washed the tattoo with salt water to keep it clean and massaged it. When his skin was fully healed, he was a man.

Samoan Women's Tattoos

Samoan women were also tattooed. The patterns were simple. Instead of heavy solid bands of tattoo, they got designs that resembled lace or flowers on their face, arms, hands, or thighs. The tattooing of women was important in the culture. A woman without tattoos on her hands would be denied the honor of serving *kava*, a special drink important for its medicinal properties, during ceremonies. Both men and women showed their commitment to their culture by getting tattoos.

The Land of the Long White Cloud

The Polynesians who arrived in the land that is today known as New Zealand called it *Aotearoa*, Land of the Long White

In this 1908 picture, a Maori girl displays her chin tattoo and other body decorations. The sculpture behind her shows the Maori's great skill in carving wood as well as carving *moko*, or facial tattoos.

Cloud. (The Maori still call it that.) The "clouds" are the snowy peaks of the land's mountains.

The Maori people were wood carvers, and they both carved and put pigment in men's spiral facial tattoos, or *moko*. The moko was not carved at puberty but throughout a man's life. A man's body was also tattooed with spiral patterns, but these were not carved.

As with Samoans, undergoing tattooing was a test of bravery, as pieces of bone, shell, or metal were dipped in pigments and hammered repeatedly into the skin. The danger of infection was great. But a man who refused to be tattooed was a "bare face." People didn't respect him.

Although mokos all looked similar, each was different. After Europeans came to New Zealand, Maori men would draw their moko as their signature on documents. As with other tattoos, the different designs had different meanings. One spiral was an opening fern and signaled a new beginning. It said something about the man's future. Another spiral represented a belly button. It meant that the man had a good, solid foundation. It was a statement about his past. The *tohunga-ta-moko*, the tattooist who chose these designs, was greatly respected.

The Meaning of Moko

Missionaries said the moko was the work of the devil. Anthropologists said they were just supposed to make the wearer attractive to the opposite sex, or make the warrior more frightening to his enemies. Certainly, war was important in Maori culture.

A dead man's head would be preserved by his family or by the enemies who killed him if he wore the *moko*. Europeans called tattoos barbaric yet were fascinated by them.

Before a battle, warriors danced their war dance, the *haka*.

The Missionaries and the Maori

The missionaries did not have an easy time converting the Maori. One chief, named Hongi, did convert to Christianity in the late 1700s. He traveled to England to help a professor translate the Bible into the Maori language. He met King George IV, who gave him a trunk full of presents. Hongi traded these for muskets and ammunition and returned to New Zealand. His guns made him an extremely successful warrior.

Hongi's enemies could not buy many guns because guns were too expensive. Then they discovered that the traders would give them a gun for just one tattooed head. Heads with *moko* were in great demand by rich collectors and museums in Europe. When the supply of people with tattooed heads ran out, the Maori began capturing and killing slaves and other men who were too low in status to have been tattooed, and they tattooed these people's heads after their death.

When stories about the trading of guns for tattooed heads got into newspapers in Europe, the British government was embarrassed into outlawing the sale of tattooed heads in 1830. Eventually, the tradition of moko died out.

Today, some Maori are reviving their tattoo tradition. Their mokos can no longer celebrate their bravery in battles, yet their mokos still accomplish one of the traditional functions of tattoos, which is to show people's identity. Their mokos now say: I am proud to be Maori.

The haka was meant to frighten their enemies but also to put them in the right mood for battle, as a team cheer prepares a school baseball team for the "battle" about to take place on the diamond.

In their myth about the beginning of tattooing, the Maori say that long ago, an ancestor had an argument with his wife. She was so angry that she left him and went to live with her father in the afterlife. The man followed her and asked her father, who was carving decorations on his house, to paint him with the same beautiful designs that he was carving. After these designs washed away in the rain, the father carved them into the man's face, making them permanent. The wife saw the beauty of the designs and recognized what great pain her husband had suffered, and she forgave him.

Yet, to say that a moko was simply intended to impress the ladies or scare the enemy does not capture what the tattoo meant to the people who wore it. The missionaries said the Maori were heathens, meaning they believed in the wrong gods. Outsiders who studied tattooing sometimes missed the religious meaning completely. Many indigenous peoples have no word for "religion." But the Maori and other Polynesians believed that a person's *mana*, their spiritual power or life force, is displayed by their tattoo. They believed that the tattooist entered an altered state of consciousness while he worked. He was in something like a trance. The unseen and mysterious powers of the universe aided him. They guided him in his choice of patterns.

Even after a man died, his moko was important. If he was killed in battle and his enemies took his head, they would display it with pride. A head without tattoos had no value. If a man's family had possession of his tattooed head, they kept it in a place of honor and took it down on ceremonial occasions.

Hawaii

Hawaii was among the last places the Polynesian culture spread. To get there, the Polynesians had to cross a whole ocean. When James Cook landed there in 1778, he was the first European to see the Hawaiian Islands. Unlike some of the other Pacific Island cultures he had seen, Hawaii had a strong hierarchy: there was a lot of control exercised by people who had the most status and the most power. Tattoos identified kings. Not everyone had them. Cook found the tattoos less elaborate than others he had seen.

Forty years later, tattooing had become more common and more elaborate. Women's tattoos included images of European animals and objects, from goats to cannons. Yet, tattoos also had some of their old meanings. Some gave magical protection. A warrior's tattoos protected him during battle.

Tattooing in Hawaii was also used during mourning. A man might tattoo his wife's name on his chest after her death. A woman wore the date of her husband's death on her arms and on the soles of her feet. She was also tattooed on the tongue—a painful process. This was an expression of her emotional pain at her loss. She literally embodied—made part of her body—her grief.

CHAPTER 4

Tattoos in Melanesia

In Melanesia, a group of islands in the Pacific Ocean northeast of Australia, people were darker skinned than the Polynesians. As in Africa and Australia, very dark-skinned people often practiced decorative scarification (made cicatrices) and body painting. In Melanesia, they also had tattoos, especially the women. Most often, these were abstract designs and images of fish, birds, and the sun and moon. Birds were related to spirits and ghosts because of their ability to fly.

Papua New Guinea

In Papua New Guinea, there is a legend that said, long ago, tattooing did not hurt. Then one day, a woman tattooing some girls passed gas, and the girls laughed. Tattooing is a serious business, and this was terribly disrespectful to the tattooist. After that, the tattooist used thorny twigs to prick the tattoos and this hurt a lot. No one would be likely to laugh at a tattooist again.

In Papua New Guinea, women rather than men wore elaborate tattoos. A woman could be tattooed from head to toe, but she would receive her tattoos at various stages throughout her life.

In most traditions, bearing pain is an important part of the process of being tattooed. Being an adult required bravery.

In Papua New Guinea, women had to be tattooed before they could be married. Beginning with a few small tattoos on their arms when they were six years old, they would then be tattooed on the chin and nose, from the belly button to the crotch, and on the inside of their thighs, armpits, and throat. At puberty, their shoulders, back, and buttocks were tattooed. Only when a woman was engaged to be married did she receive the chevrons (V shapes) on her chest. Older women applied these tattoos. Neither the older woman, nor the family member in charge of holding the girl still, nor the girl herself was allowed, by tradition, to make a sound.

Men had smaller and fewer tattoos. These served several functions. They were used to relieve pain at the joints and in the heart. They marked great achievements, such as leading a long journey by boat to trade with another island or killing an enemy.

Borneo

The tattoo traditions of Borneo survived the periods of history when outsiders destroyed many cultures and their traditions. Borneo is the third-biggest island in the world (Greenland and New Guinea are bigger). Its mountains and rainforests kept outsiders from reaching the island's inland. It is an ancient land of many tribes. Many of these are grouped together and called Dayaks, but they were different from one another.

Their tradition was communal. Large numbers of family groups—as many as sixty—shared huge thatched structures. But warfare between tribes was fierce. Tradition said that tattoos would help people after they died. Tattoos on the hand were a sign of high status in life. After the person died, the hand tattoo would light the person's way as his or her soul searched for the River of the Dead. The spirit guarding the river looked for this tattoo on the souls that approached it. Only a soul with the hand tattoo could safely cross the river to

This Dayak noblewoman from Borneo wears the hand tattoos that will enable her to travel safely to the afterlife.

the afterlife. The soul of a warrior who had died fighting had a special place there, where he could live in comfort without working. But without the tattoo, the soul would be drowned in the river. Maggots would eat it.

Traditional Dayak tattoos were applied first as designs stamped onto the skin with carved blocks of wood. The tattooist would then prick the skin, forcing the pigment underneath. Today, their tattoos look like abstract patterns or stars, but the Dayaks recognized them as animals, including scorpions, shrimp, and dogs. Because the blocks were used many times and traded, many men had some of the same tattoos. Also, the men collected tattoos when they traveled among allies.

Because they did not travel widely, the tattoos of women and girls were more distinct by tribe. Their tattoos were applied very gradually over a period of about four years, between about the ages of ten and fourteen. The tattoos had to be finished before the woman became pregnant.

A Dayak healing ritual suggests an origin for one meaning of a tattoo. The

In Borneo, as on other Pacific islands, young men and women today are being tattooed with patterns like the ones their ancestors wore.

design tattooed on the wrist is called *lukat*, which is a bead used in a healing ritual. The Dayaks believed that sick people's souls leave their bodies. If the people recovered, their souls had returned, and they tied a lukat on their wrists to "tie in" the soul. The tattooed image of the bead serves the same purpose but cannot be lost. As in many places, the tattoo is a permanent jewel. The belief may seem odd, but a pulse beating in the wrist shows that someone is alive.

CHAPTER 5

Lost Traditions of North America

The tattoo traditions of the Americas have mostly been lost or misunderstood. In 1615, a French explorer named Gabriel Sagard-Théodat described the process of tattooing among the Huron, a people of what is now eastern Canada. As reported in *Tattoo History*, he wrote that it was "a most strange and conspicuous folly" intended to make them "considered courageous and feared by their enemies." He described a process by which the Huron remained silent and still while his body was punctured with a sharpened bone and "black color" was rubbed in. Missionaries reported seeing tattooing among other tribes and agreed it was a "bizarre custom." At least one traveler, the Frenchman Jean Bernard Bossu, disagreed.

Bossu Among the Osage

In the mid-1700s, Bossu stayed with the Osage Indians for several months, in what is now Alabama. As described in *Tattoo History*, Bossu wrote that the Osages tattooed a deer on his thigh, saying he was their brother and that as he traveled among the tribes who were their allies, he could show his tattoo, smoke a peace pipe, and be welcomed.

Getting the tattoo hurt, but Bossu understood that he needed to show his bravery. He joked with people who were watching. They told him he was a "real man."

Bossu told the story of an Osage man who got a tattoo he hadn't earned. A man who had never fought a battle got a tomahawk tattoo to impress a woman he wanted to marry. Tribal leaders said they would cut it off his body. (Instead, Bossu mixed opium, a narcotic drug, to deaden the pain and an insect-based blistering agent, and he was able to remove the man's tattoo, along with his skin.)

For the Osages, tattoos identified friends from foes, and they showed a man's battle records. In addition, the act of bearing the pain of getting the tattoo showed bravery. The Osages tattooed Bossu with a picture of a deer, which might have meant that he had a special connection with people whose totem was the deer. A totem is an animal, plant, or other natural object that is sacred to a group of people.

Other Meanings of North American Tattoos

In other tribal nations, the tattoo was part of the rites of passage at puberty. They were used in curing rituals to relieve pain. One old warrior of the Lenape people was tattooed with scenes of every battle he'd been in. For other peoples, this record might be kept painted on animal hides instead of tattooed into their

This Iroquois man, drawn in 1701, wears tattoos that probably show his clan (the people of the turtle) and his military accomplishments.

own skin. Warriors might be tattooed with a symbol that represented every enemy they had killed, or this information could be marked in paint on their warhorse as they went into battle, or by the wearing of enemy scalps sewn on a shirt. So, important information about the person could be noted and displayed in different ways.

It is always difficult for us to know all of what tattoos meant to the native peoples who wore them. In 1878, James G. Swan, from Boston, wrote in his book *Tattoo Marks of the Haida* about the tattoos of the Haida, a Northwest coast people. The Haida allowed Swan to copy their tattoo designs. These were, as for the Maori and some other peoples with strong traditions of wood carving, similar to designs used in carving their renowned totem poles. The Haida told him that these designs of stylized animals were family crests and totem marks. The Haida differed from most other groups in that they used something (he didn't name it) to deaden the skin. Although getting a tattoo was still painful, bearing pain was a less important part of the ceremony for many peoples.

Yet, Swan knew he didn't have the whole explanation for what the tattoos meant. The images were so stylized that he could not even recognize them, although the Haida easily understood them. Everyone he asked could identify the tattoo of a hummingbird or a codfish. But he didn't know, in a deeper sense, what they meant. He knew that there was a connection between the tattoo designs

The design on the forehead of this painted and carved mask looks like abstract art to an outsider but was a specific animal to the Haida.

and the myths of the people, but these were not matters that they would talk to an outsider about.

The Inuit and Arctic Peoples

We know more about the tattoos of Arctic peoples, such as the Inuit living in Alaska, northern Canada, and Greenland. Theirs

dess et Lith par Choris

In the far north, in what are now Alaska and Greenland, tattoo designs were "sewn in" under the skin.

is an ancient tradition. A small carving from 3,500 years ago shows a human face with patterns that are probably tattoos. Because of these peoples' relative isolation, the tradition survived until recently and is now being revived.

Inuit tattoos were applied in a different way from most others: they were sewn in. The tattooists were mostly older women with much experience sewing clothing and household goods made of animals hides. To make tattoos, they used a needle to draw a pigment-soaked thread through the surface of the person's skin. The pigment was made of graphite and urine. Both were believed to have the power to protect people against evil spirits. The urine would also have functioned as an antibiotic.

Like the Dayaks in Borneo, the Inuit believed that people's souls depart when they are ill. "Soul" here does not mean exactly what it does for Christians. Instead, the "soul" is the person's warmth, breath, and physical senses. These are the things that most obviously make a living person different from a dead body. The soul of the dead person is understood to leave only gradually. In a rite of passage from childhood to adulthood, there is a time when the person is no longer a child but is not yet an adult. Transitional times are dangerous. There is a time when the person is dead, but the spirit has not gone far and may infect the living. The Inuit people who carried the body to its burial place were tattooed for protection at their joints, the places where the dead person's soul might enter them. For the same reason, men were tattooed the first time they killed a seal, polar bear, or whale. The dead animal, like the dead person, had a soul that could infect them.

What Do Tattoos Mean?

Whe Joseph Banks, the English naturalist aboard Captain Cook's ship bound for Tahiti, saw his first tattoos, he was confused. He understood that some small marks might just be for beauty. After all, women in England at that time applied fake "beauty marks" to their faces. But when he saw a fourteen-year-old girl getting tattooed on her buttocks, he couldn't understand it at all. "What can be sufficient inducement to suffer so much pain is difficult to say," he wrote in his journal. "Possibly superstition may have something to do with it; nothing else in my opinion could be sufficient cause for apparently so absurd a custom."

Sometimes, it's easy to understand indigenous cultures and their tattoos. The Osage Indian mentioned earlier got a tomahawk tattoo to impress his girlfriend. At other times, a little more information is needed. If you learned in a first aid course that it's better to urinate on a wound than to put it in an unknown water supply, then you are less surprised that the Inuit and others use urine as a disinfectant, even though it is also body waste. But often it is impossible to know what something means without knowing a great deal about the people. You may feel that some of the beliefs of indigenous peoples are really very strange. *You* are not so superstitious and unscientific—except when you wear your lucky socks to take an exam, or insist on taking antibiotics when you have a virus.

Science is only one of the tools that modern people use to understand their world. Indigenous peoples also use different tools in understanding the world. They may pass down through the years the knowledge of which herbs will treat an illness, but also know that after a long illness a person needs to be reunited with the everyday world and with his or her community. That ceremony, sometimes including a tattoo, is a cure as well as the herb.

You can understand how other people recognize very abstract designs if you look at some of the ones you use. The emoticons in e-mails make perfect sense to people who are used to them. To an outsider, they are mysterious. How can a few little dots mean anything?

You can better understand how tattoos unite, divide, or identify different groups if you think about how an item of modern body decoration identifies people in your school. What would happen to some sorry visitor from another country who thought that he could wear the varsity football team's letter jacket because he liked the way it looked or because it seemed (to use the anthropologist's language) to "confer status" upon the people who wore it? Someone might tear the thing off his

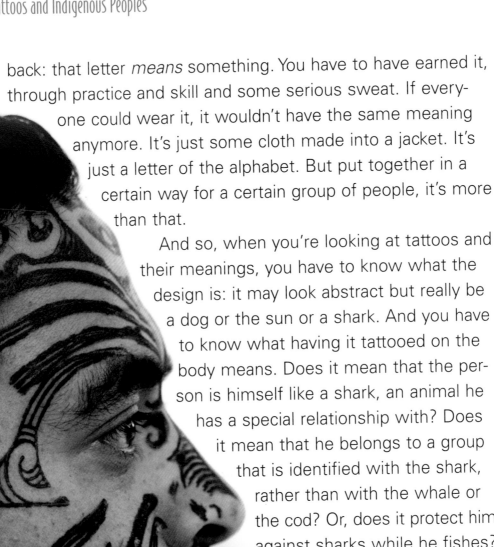

back: that letter *means* something. You have to have earned it, through practice and skill and some serious sweat. If everyone could wear it, it wouldn't have the same meaning anymore. It's just some cloth made into a jacket. It's just a letter of the alphabet. But put together in a certain way for a certain group of people, it's more than that.

And so, when you're looking at tattoos and their meanings, you have to know what the design is: it may look abstract but really be a dog or the sun or a shark. And you have to know what having it tattooed on the body means. Does it mean that the person is himself like a shark, an animal he has a special relationship with? Does it mean that he belongs to a group that is identified with the shark, rather than with the whale or the cod? Or, does it protect him against sharks while he fishes?

Tattoos were and are used in many ways by indigenous peoples. Typically, they are for

This modern Maori cannot head-hunt as his ancestors did, but he can wear a *moko*, showing his pride in his heritage. The tattoo says: I am Maori.

beauty reasons. Usually, people remained silent to show their bravery, although boys of the Marquesas Islands in Polynesia were supposed to yell so that everyone would appreciate what great pain they were enduring. It is a mark of pride if the person has chosen it, or it has been chosen for that person by someone he or she respects. But it can also be used for punishment. Tattoos can give magic protection.

A tattoo shows who someone is. Like the high school varsity jacket, or the symbol of your religion, it shows someone's membership in a group.

Some tribal peoples would prefer to keep it that way. Their traditions have been destroyed or almost destroyed by outsiders. Their tattoos were forbidden. People started to be ashamed of them. Today, some people in the Polynesian Islands, Borneo, and the Arctic are getting the tattoos of their ancestors and are bringing the traditions back to life. But now, other people who don't know about their cultures are interested in the tattoos, too. The "tribal" armband was a Samoan answer to that interest, designed to give American Peace Corps workers a souvenir and a "thank you" for their work in

Modern tribal-style tattoos are often handsome but do not make the same kind of statement about the wearer's identity that a real indigenous tattoo can make.

Samoa. It looks Samoan, but is not a real tradition. Tribal-*style* tattoos don't upset the indigenous peoples trying to preserve their heritage, but when a Web site once offered for sale fake mokos as creepy Halloween masks, the Maori were seriously offended. Tattoos, like letter jackets or religious symbols, can only keep their meaning when people who know what they mean wear them. They're not just a style, not just one more thing for people to buy.

 Glossary

adaption The process of adjusting to environmental conditions.

anthropologist A scientist who studies the social and cultural behavior of groups of human beings.

archaeologist A scientist who recovers and studies the material evidence from human life and culture in past ages.

barbarian A person who is considered to be primitive, rude, or violent.

Crusader Someone who participated in the Christian military missions of the eleventh through thirteenth centuries intended to take Jerusalem and the Holy Land from the Muslims then living there.

excavate To dig up scientifically in order to study what is dug up.

fortitude The strength that makes someone able to bear pain or trouble bravely.

myth Often used to mean "lie" or untrue story, a myth is also the most deeply true and important stories of a culture that explain what the gods want them to understand.

nomad Member of a cultural group that moves from place to place according to the season, sometimes to find pastures for its animals.

pigment A substance used to dye or color something.

pilgrim A member of a religion who travels to a holy place or who takes a trip for religious reasons, as when Europeans came to North America to practice their religion.

steppes Very large, dry plains.

superstition An irrational belief held by someone else; we call our own superstitions "beliefs."

totem An animal, plant, or other natural object, such as a stone or river, that is sacred for a group of people and is their symbol. The word can also be used to describe the group of people who are united by that symbol.

tribal tattoo A contemporary abstract or geometric design for the skin that is copied or adapted from the tattoo designs of indigenous peoples.

tufuga The craftsperson of Samoa who gave Samoans their tattoos during traditional rituals.

For More Information

Center for World Indigenous Studies
PMB 214-1001 Cooper Point Road SW, Suite 140
Olympia, WA 98501
(360) 586-0656
Web site: http://www.cwis.org
This research and educational organization is helping to lead to a wider
understanding of the ideas and knowledge of indigenous peoples and to
give information about what their current lives are like.

National Museum of the American Indian
George Gustav Heye Center
U.S. Custom House
One Bowling Green
New York, NY 10004
(212) 514-3700
Web site: http://www.nmai.si.edu

**National Museum of the American Indian
on the National Mall**
Fourth Street and Independence Avenue SW
Washington, DC 20560
(202) 633-1000
Web site: http://www.nmai.si.edu
The National Museums of the American Indian are branches of the
Smithsonian Institution. They have exhibitions, public events, and libraries
devoted to the native peoples of the United States.

National Tattoo Association
485 Business Park Lane
Allentown, PA 18109
(610) 433-7261
Web site: http://www.nationaltattooassociation.com
The National Tattoo Association operates an annual convention that has been running for twenty-eight years.

The Tattoo Archive
618 West 4th Street
Winston-Salem, NC 27101
(366) 722-4422
Web site: http://www.tattooarchive.com
The Tattoo Archive encompasses a design museum, a research center, and a bookstore.

Web Sites

Due to the changing nature of Internet links, Rosen Publishing has developed an online list of Web sites related to the subject of this book. This site is updated regularly. Please use this link to access the list:

http://www.rosenlinks.com/ttt/toip

FOR FURTHER READING

Bankston, John. *Margaret Mead: Pioneer of Social Anthropology.* Berkeley Heights, NJ: Enslow, 2006.

Batten, Mary. *Anthropologist: Scientist of the People.* Boston, MA: Houghton Mifflin, 2001.

Corbin, George C. *The Native Arts of North America, Africa and the South Pacific: An Introduction.* New York, NY: HarperCollins, 1988.

Currie-McGhee, Leanne K. *Tattoos and Body Piercing.* Detroit, MI: Lucent Books, 2006.

Flood, Bo, Berret E. Strong, William Flood, and Connie Jo Adams. *Pacific Island Legends: Tales from Micronesia, Melanesia, Polynesia, and Australia.* Honolulu, HI: Bess Press, 1999.

Gay, Kathlyn, and Christine Whittington. *Body Marks: Tattooing, Piercing, and Scarification.* Brookfield, CT: 21st Century, 2002.

Mason, Paul. *Tattoos and Body Piercings.* Portsmouth, NH: Heinemann Library, 2003.

Meltzer, Milton. *Captain James Cook.* New York, NY: Benchmark Books/Marshall Cavendish, 2002.

Philip, Neil. *The Great Circle: A History of the First Nations.* New York, NY: Clarion, 2006.

Sharpe, Anne. *The Pacific Islands* (Indigenous Peoples of the World). Detroit, MI: Lecent Books, 2002.

BIBLIOGRAPHY

Bossu, Jean Bernard. *Travels in the Interior of North America, 1751–1762.* Translated by Seymour Feller, 1962. Excerpted in Steve Gilbert, *Tattoo History: A Source Book.* New York, NY: Juno Books, 2000.

Darwin, Charles. *The Descent of Man.* New York, NY: Appleton and Co., 1883.

DeMarban, Alex. "Symbols on Skin Connect Hearts to History Alaska." *Anchorage Daily News*, September 17, 2006. Retrieved August 16, 2007 (http://www.adn.com/news/alaska/rural/story/8204564p-8098495c.html).

DeMello, Margo. *Bodies of Inscription: A Cultural History of the Modern Tattoo Community.* Durham, NC: Duke University Press, 2000.

Geertz, Clifford. *The Interpretation of Cultures.* New York, NY: Basic Books, 1973.

Gilbert, Steve, ed. *Tattoo History: A Source Book.* New York, NY: Juno Books, 2000.

Hesselt van Dinter, Maarten. *The World of Tattoos: An Illustrated History.* Amsterdam, Netherlands: KIT Publishers, 2005.

Lineberry, Cate. "Tattoos: The Ancient and Mysterious History." Smithsonian.com, January 1, 2007. Retrieved August 16, 2007 (http://www.smithsonianmagazine.com/issues/2007/january/tattoo.htm).

Marquardt, Carl. *Die Tätowierung Beider Geschlechter in Samoa.* Berlin, Germany: Dietrich Reimer, 1899. Translated by Sybil

Ferner as *The Tattooing of Both Sexes in Samoa*. Papakura, New Zealand: R. McMillan, 1984.

Sagard-Théodat, Gabriel. Quoted in Philippe Dubé, *Tattoo-tatoué*. Montreal, Canada: Jean Basile, 1960. Cited in Steve Gilbert, *Tattoo History: A Source Book*. New York, NY: Juno Books, 2000.

"Skin Stories: The Art and Culture of Polynesian Tattoo." PBS.org. Retrieved November 29, 2007 (http://www.pbs.org/skinstories).

Stocking, George W., Jr., ed. *A Franz Boas Reader: The Shaping of American Anthropology 1883–1911*. New York, NY: Basic Books, 1974.

Swan, James G. "Tattoo Marks of the Haida" (1878). Excerpted in Steve Gilbert, *Tattoo History: A Source Book*. New York, NY: Juno Books, 2000.

Van Gennep, Arnold. *The Rites of Passage*. Chicago, IL: University of Chicago Press, 1960.

Index

About the Author

Judith Levin is the author of numerous books for children and young adults, many of them about people of other cultures. She has published books about Hammurabi, the ancient Mesopotamian king; Ichiro, the Japanese baseball player; and Japanese mythology. She coauthored a book about Tenochtitlan. Levin completed graduate coursework in folklore at the University of Pennsylvania.

Photo Credits

Designer: Les Kanturek; **Editor:** Kathy Kuhtz Campbell;
Photo Researcher: Cindy Reiman